*HABITATS OF* *THE WORLD*

# DESERTS

### Written and Illustrated by
## Sheri Amsel

A LUCAS • EVANS BOOK

RSVP
**RAINTREE STECK-VAUGHN**
P U B L I S H E R S
The Steck-Vaughn Company

*Austin, Texas*

For my parents

**Consultant:**   James G. Doherty, General Curator, Bronx Zoo, Bronx, New York

**Book Design:**  M 'N O Production Services, Inc.

**Library of Congress Cataloging-in-Publication Data**

Amsel, Sheri.
   Deserts / written and illustrated by Sheri Amsel.
     p.   cm. — (Habitats of the world)
   "A Lucas/Evans book."
   Includes index.
   Summary: Discusses the plant and animal life of the world's deserts and the need to conserve the earth's natural desert resources.
   ISBN 0-8114-6300-1
   1. Deserts biology—Juvenile literature.   2. Deserts—Juvenile literature.
[1. Desert biology.   2. Deserts.]   I. Title.
II. Series: Amsel, Sheri. Habitats of the world.
QH88.A48   1993
574.909'54—dc20                       92-8789
                                              CIP
                                              AC

Printed and bound in the United States.

1 2 3 4 5 6 7 8 9 0  VH  98 97 96 95 94 93

# Table of Contents

# DESERTS OF THE WORLD

When you think of deserts, do you think of a dry, hot, endless sea of sand, devoid of life? It is true that deserts are dry, and during the day when temperatures may soar above 100 degrees Fahrenheit, they can be too hot to walk on, even with shoes. At midday the scorching sun overhead burns fiercely. A shimmer of heat rises from the rocks and sand. But at night the desert can be cold, and the temperature can drop well below freezing. Still most deserts are actually full of life. To live in the desert, however, plants and animals have to develop many special tricks, or adaptations, to survive these extreme temperatures and the lack of water.

Deserts get rainfall, but not on a regular basis and often not enough to soak the ground. Sometimes a sudden heavy rain will fall and cause flash floods. A very dry riverbed can become a rushing river in only a few minutes. On the other hand, some of the world's deserts wait years and years for a rainfall. In the Atacama Desert in South America, there has never been a recorded rainfall. Mostly though, deserts receive at least occasional rain.

Every year the deserts are growing. Moisture determines whether an area is an arid grassland or a desert. Many grasslands subsist on just a few more inches of regular rainfall than a neighboring desert. A change of conditions can often push a grassland into more of a desert. That is what has happened in many grasslands throughout the world where people allow their domestic animals to overgraze. The roots of plants and grasses hold moisture and stabilize the soil. When they are eaten away, the topsoil dries up and is either blown or washed away. The land becomes a desert.

Rainfall brings a sudden bloom of desert life. Some plants quickly flower and make new seeds that harden and wait out the next long drought. With the new plant life to eat, animals will have more young. Most animals here are active at night. They also hunt for food in the early morning hours before it gets too hot, then escape underground where it is cooler when temperatures rise. Desert life expands with rain, only to die back again as the water dwindles and no new rain falls.

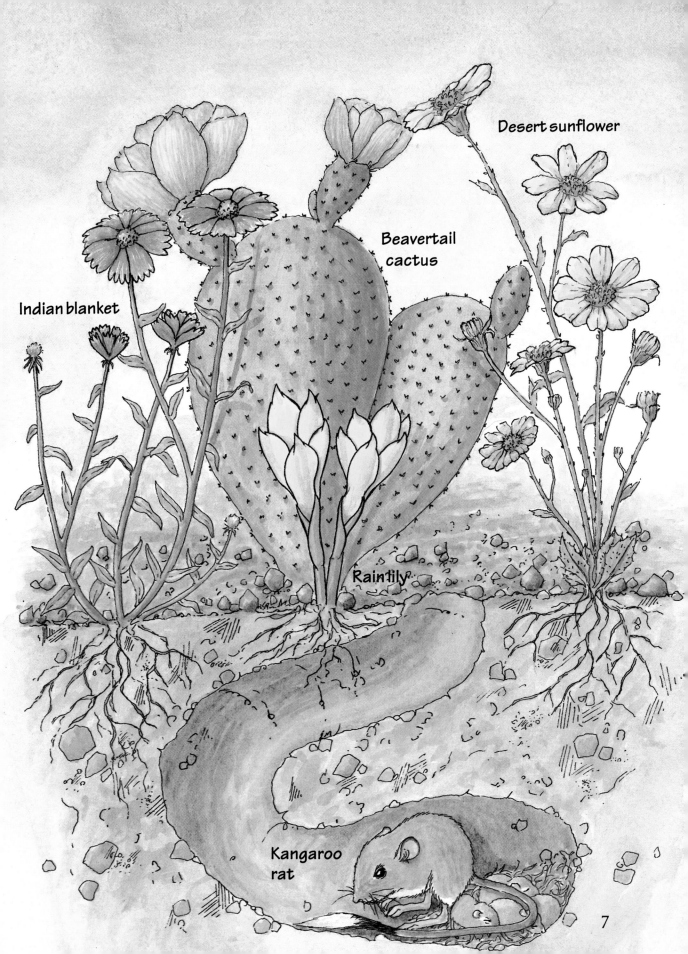

Desert sunflower

Beavertail
cactus

Indian blanket

Rain lily

Kangaroo
rat

# Deserts of North America

The Sonoran Desert is one of large sandy plains and bleak mountains. It stretches over parts of southern California, Arizona, and northwestern Mexico. Branches of the Colorado River run through it, so many trees, large cacti, and shrubs find enough water to grow here.

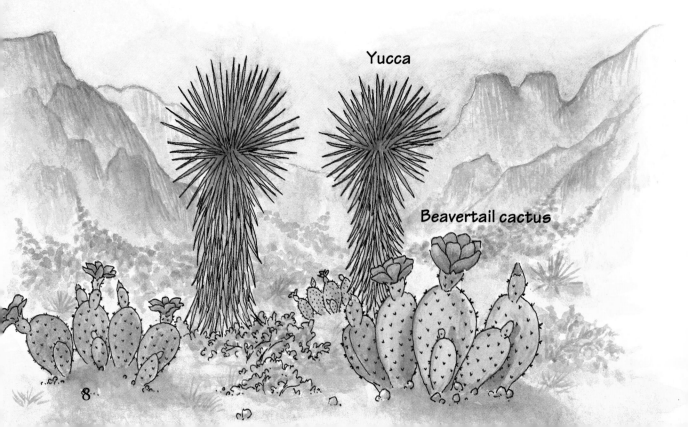

Yucca

Beavertail cactus

Palo verde

Mesquite

Creosote
bush

Saguaro
cactus

Barrel cactus

Yucca

In Arizona the giant saguaro cactus and the barrel cactus are quite
plentiful. Mesquite and creosote bush also do well here, and after a
rain the hillsides can be ablaze with the yellow blossoms of palo verde.
Beautiful flowering cacti and yucca make the desert seem more like
a garden than the open sandy space one might imagine.

Joshua tree

$N$orth of the Sonoran Desert is the small Mojave Desert. It is known for its vast stands of Joshua trees. This cactus-like tree is a yucca and not a cactus at all. It belongs to the lily family.

Death Valley cuts a swath below sea level through the Mojave. It is one of the hottest places on earth. Strange land forms and drifting sand dunes decorate this arid basin.

Remarkably, in both these deserts many animals manage to thrive in the dry landscape. The desert jackrabbit eats such plants as the juicy cactus, carefully avoiding the sharp spines. Its long ears pick up the slightest sound of danger. They also help to cool off the jackrabbit's furry body by allowing excess body heat to escape through many delicate blood vessels.

The tiny kit fox also cools off by using its huge ears. Its sharp hearing helps as it hunts for insects, rodents, and other small animals.

Kit fox

Jackrabbit

Desert tortoise

The oldest animal on the desert may be the desert tortoise. Legally protected now from humans who collected these scarce turtles for their shells, meat, or to sell as pets, they roam the dry land eating the tough shrubs, grasses, and cacti.

A damp hole in a saguaro cactus helps a family of elf owls keep cool. At night these birds will fly out in search of insects to eat.

On the ground a Gambel's quail searches for seeds and insects.

In the sky, a turkey vulture makes large, slow circles in its constant search for carrion.

Turkey vulture

Elf owl

Gambel's quail

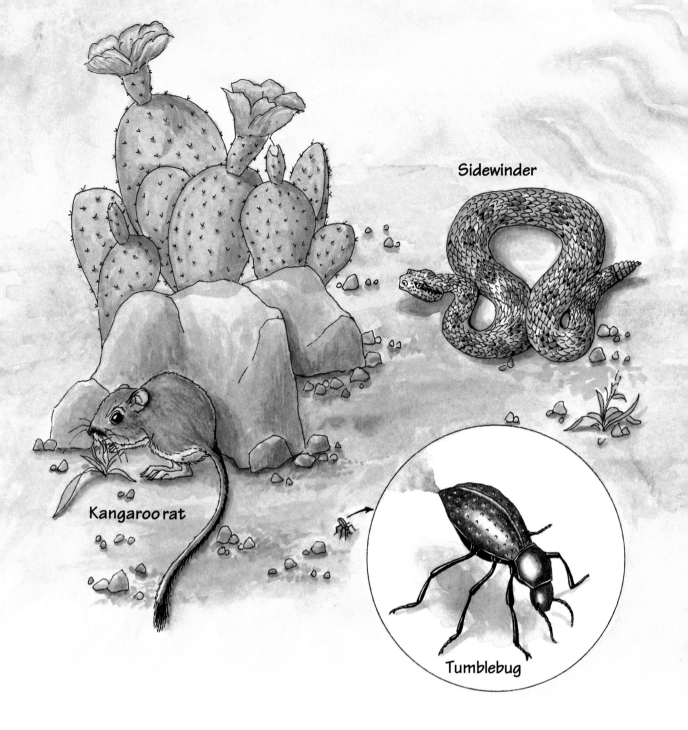

Sidewinder

Kangaroo rat

Tumblebug

$S$kidding across the sand, a deadly sidewinder leaves a strange
warning trail. A kangaroo rat springs away from its path to find a safe
hiding place. Disturbed by the fleeing rodent, a tumblebug lifts its back
to spray in case of danger. In this way, animals in the desert employ all
kinds of strange means to survive.

# The Deserts of Australia

The deserts of Australia cover about one-third of the whole country. Many of them are red sand plains with great dunes. Desert mountains, however, rise in the west like great red bluffs, and the desert lying to the south is covered with stones.

The desert lands here, like other deserts, have numerous dry lakes that shimmer from a distance as if they were full of water. This phenomenon is called a "mirage" and is actually a reflection of the sky on the superheated air just above the desert sand. Many desert travelers have been dangerously lured into the dry expanse by these visions of water far off on the plain. It is no surprise that one of the biggest dry lakes was named Lake Disappointment.

Acacia trees survive in these arid lands by having small leaves which lose little water in the dry air. The eucalyptus leaves point up and down to catch as little direct sun as possible.

Animals adapt to the lack of water as well. The koala, for example, lives entirely on the moisture it gets from eating the leaves of the eucalyptus tree.

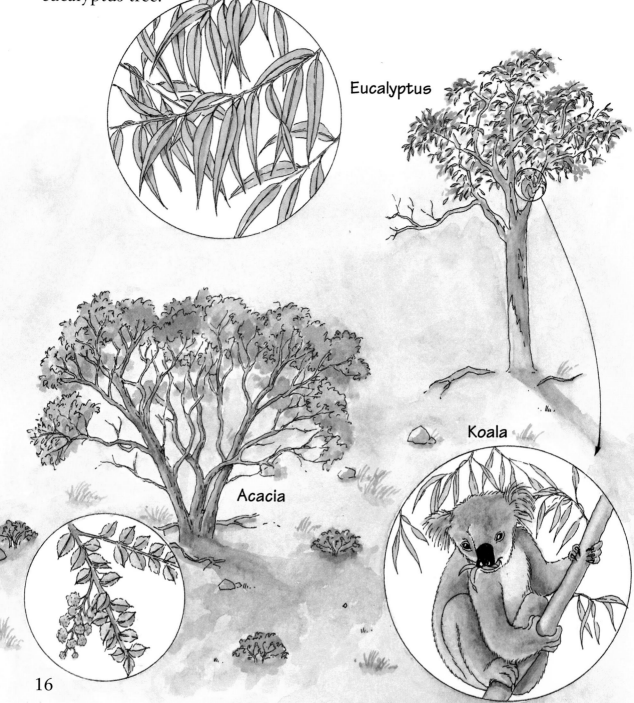

Eucalyptus

Koala

Acacia

Black cockatoo

Wedge-tailed eagle

Honeyeater

River gum

Pardalote

River gum trees survive on the fringe of the deserts or along creek beds. These are the homes for many beautiful birds. The pardalote, honeyeater, and black cockatoo bring color to the pale land. In the sky the wedge-tailed eagle, Australia's largest, soars in search of food.

Looking for insects, fruits, and tender plants, the emu range through much of Australia from desert to grassy plains. Considered a pest by farmers, emus have survived attempts to eliminate them. Their great speed carries them across many miles in search of food. The young are born with cryptic stripes that make them blend in among the grasses and shrubs.

Emu

Butcherbird

Zebra finch

$B$utcherbirds sing beautifully at dawn, but this bird, with such a lovely song, is also a ruthless hunter. When a butcherbird catches its prey, it kills it by impaling it on a sharp thorn. On the ground, flocks of zebra finches hop around in search of grass seeds.

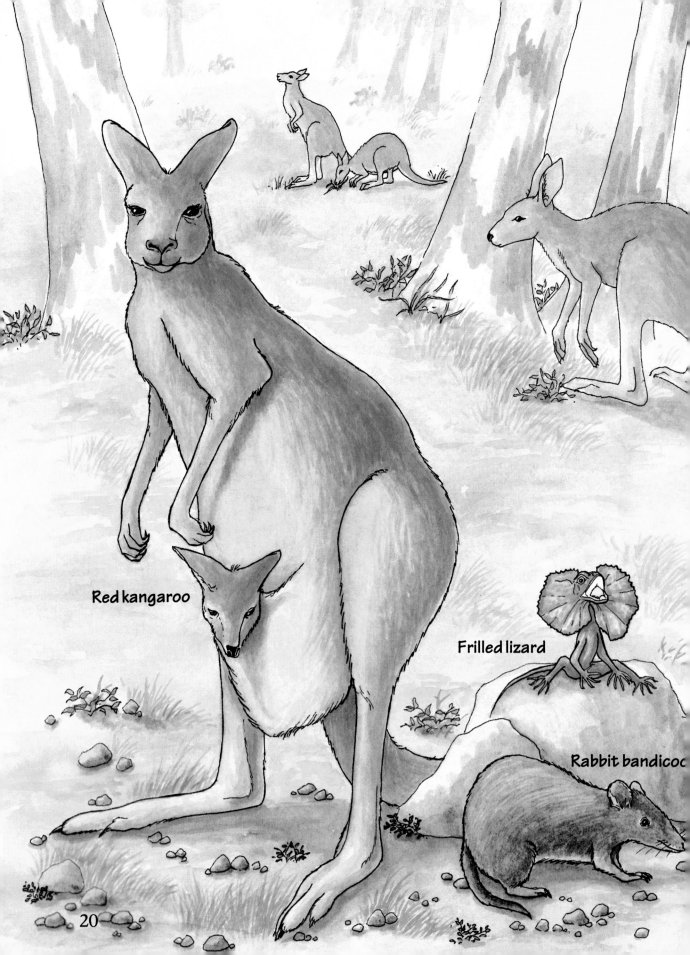

Red kangaroo

Frilled lizard

Rabbit bandicoo

Red kangaroos, traveling in groups known as mobs, can survive for days without water. They get the moisture they need from the plants they eat, and when they get hot, they pant like a dog instead of wasting precious water by sweating. Like most desert animals, kangaroos rest during the day in the mulga grass and graze in the cooler evenings. Dingos, Australia's wild dogs, travel widely through the hot plains in search of prey. Howling instead of barking, they hunt for kangaroos and other mammals.

Rabbit bandicoots dig for insects underground. Geckos and lizards search the sand and rocks for eggs, insects, and small prey. The strange frilled lizard has a giant ruff around its neck and spreads it to look larger and help scare away enemies. If it doesn't scare them, it leaps up onto its back feet and runs with all its might. Escaping predators is just as important as finding food and water.

Dingo

Gecko

# The Sahara and Namib of Africa

The Sahara is the largest desert on earth. It is as big as
the entire United States. Stretching from the Atlantic Ocean
to the Red Sea, it covers many countries in Africa. The Sahara
is one of the hottest and driest of the world's deserts with
temperatures up to 136 degrees Fahrenheit. Less than one
inch of rain falls each year. Some years the rain never comes at all.
Only creatures specially adapted for the severe conditions, like the
camel, can hope to survive here.

There are many landscapes in the Sahara. Great flat areas of gravel and stone, rocky plateaus, mountains, and vast seas of endless sand all make up this desert. The great sandy areas are called "ergs" and offer few of the things needed to sustain any kind of life. The Sahara's ergs have huge wind-blown sand dunes, some up to 600 feet tall. The greatest erg is in Libya and is as large as the whole country of France.

Camel

Small oases of water are found throughout the Sahara. In these places a few people live and even grow crops. Where water is near, herbs and small shrubs can grow. Deep rooted trees survive in wetter areas.

In the cool of the evening, the tiny fennec fox comes up from its underground tunnel to hunt desert mice, birds, and lizards. Its huge ears help it hear the smallest scurry. It has adapted well to the desert and rarely needs to drink.

Fennec fox

Gerbil

Gerbils also live underground in the heat of the day. At night they emerge to search for seeds, roots, flowers, and insects, careful to avoid the larger animals hunting them. When in danger, they stay very still. Their colors blend with the desert's, making them difficult to see. If they must escape, they use their powerful jumping legs to get a fast head start.

The beautiful addax antelope was once abundant in the Sahara. It can live without water by getting its moisture from the plants it eats. Now, because of overhunting by humans, there are few addax left and they are protected by law.

The large and handsome barbary sheep also scrape a meager existence from the desert.

Barbary sheep

Addax antelope

26

The Namib Desert rises from the southwestern coast of Africa into towering white dunes. The annual rainfall averages less than one inch. In many years rain does not fall at all. Instead, the scant moisture on the Namib comes from thick fog that rolls in off the coast at night. This is enough to sustain some hardy plant life, like the strange Welwitschia, whose leathery leaves are well-adapted to desert life. Insects and reptiles are the most customary animal residents, surviving on windblown seeds, plant particles, and each other. When fog rolls in, the head-stander beetle tips up on its head and collects the watery mist that rolls down its body into its mouth. Large mammals such as giraffes, elephants, lions, and jackals may roam the riverbed oasis when there is a bit of water.

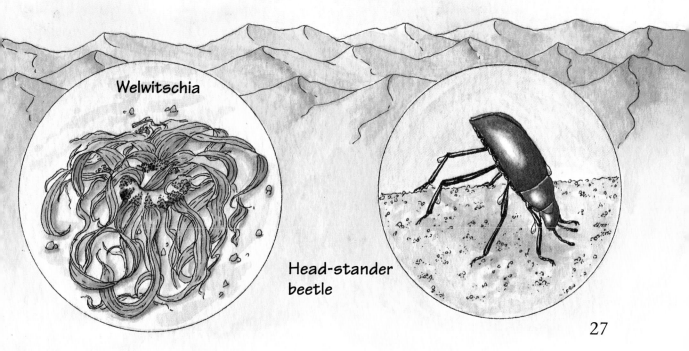

Welwitschia

Head-stander beetle

# The Gobi Desert

The Gobi Desert is a windswept and treeless plain that extends from southern Mongolia to northern China. It is mostly rock, with none of the usual sandy dunes one would expect in a desert. In some parts of the Gobi, feather grass, snakeweed, and other plants survive the heat and drought. They provide food for wild camels and the kulan that still roam the rugged land.

People roam the Gobi with herds of sheep, cattle, and goats, in search of the scant vegetation. But their numbers are few, and they must keep on the move to find enough food.

Kulan

Feather grass

# Deserts Today

As human populations grow, the need for space and resources has sent developers, people who build or exploit resources, into the deserts more and more. Minerals and oil are mined, and if the land is not too dry, it is often irrigated and farmed! Animals are collected for sale as pets or hunted as food. So even a land that would seem protected by its own harsh ways, can be destroyed by humans. As with all natural habitats, the desert needs protection, too.

Wild camel

# Glossary

**adaptation:** traits developed to make a plant or animal more fit to survive and reproduce

**bluff:** a high, steep bank or cliff

**carrion:** dead and decaying animal flesh

**cryptic:** meant to conceal

**developer:** people that make natural areas more usable to humans

**drought:** a long spell of dry weather

**erg:** a large, uninterrupted expanse of desert land

**flash flood:** a sudden, overwhelming surge of water usually resulting from heavy rain upstream, or at the flood site

**graze:** to feed on grass or pasture

**habitat:** the place where a plant or animal is naturally found

**mirage:** a visual illusion above a superheated surface

**oasis:** a fertile area in a dry, arid region

**overgraze:** to overfeed on a pasture, depleting its grassy cover

**plateau:** a large, level area raised above the surrounding land

**predator:** an animal that lives by killing and consuming other animals

**prey:** an animal taken for food by another

**rodent:** any of a large group of small mammals with sharp front teeth used for gnawing

# Animals Index

# Plants Index

| DATE DUE | | | |
|----------|--|--|--|
|  |  |  |  |
|  |  |  |  |
|  |  |  |  |
|  |  |  |  |
|  |  |  |  |
|  |  |  |  |
|  |  |  |  |
|  |  |  |  |
|  |  |  |  |
|  |  |  |  |

574.909    Amsel, Sheri.
Ams
         Deserts